(

O(

DEC

I'm Good At

I'm Good at Math

Eileen M. Day

Heinemann Library

Chicago, Illinois

Designed by Sue Emerson, Heinemann Library; Page layout by Que-Net Media
Printed and bound in the United States by Lake Book Manufacturing, Inc.
Photo research by Alan Gottlieb and Amor Montes de Oca

07 06 05 04 03
10 9 8 7 6 5 4 3 2 1

Library of Congress Cataloging-in-Publication Data
Day, Eileen.
 I'm good at math / Eileen Day.
      p. cm. — (I'm good at)
Includes index.
Summary: Explains what mathematics is and how it feels to do math, and shows some basic mathematical concepts such as sorting and measuring.

 ISBN 1-4034-0901-3 (HC), 1-4034-3448-4 (Pbk.)
 1. Mathematics—Juvenile literature. [1. Mathematics.] I. Title. II. Series.
 QA40.5 .D39 2003
 510—dc21

                         2002014734

Acknowledgments
The author and publishers are grateful to the following for permission to reproduce copyrighted material:
p. 4 Stephen McBrady/Photo Edit; pp. 5, 6, 7, 8, 9, 10, 11, 12, 14, 15, 17, 19, 22, 23, 24, back cover Robert Lifson/Heinemann Library; p. 13 Russell D. Curtis/Photo Researchers, Inc.; p. 16 Jose Luis Pelaez, Inc./Corbis; p. 18 Stone/Getty Images; p. 20 Bob Daemmrich/Stock Boston; p. 21 Bob Daemmrich Photography, Inc

Cover photograph by Tom & Dee Ann McCarthy/Corbis

Every effort has been made to contact copyright holders of any material reproduced in this book. Any omissions will be rectified in subsequent printings if notice is given to the publisher.

Special thanks to our advisory panel for their help in the preparation of this book:

Alice Bethke,
Library Consultant
Palo Alto, CA

Kathleen Gilbert,
Second Grade Teacher
Round Rock, TX

Sandra Gilbert,
Library Media Specialist
Fiest Elementary School
Houston, TX

Jan Gobeille,
Kindergarten Teacher
Garfield Elementary
Oakland, CA

Angela Leeper,
Educational Consultant
North Carolina Department
of Public Instruction
Wake Forest, NC

Some words are shown in bold, **like this.**
You can find them in the picture glossary on page 23.

Contents

What Is Math?

Math is using numbers and symbols.

Some numbers tell how much things cost.

Other numbers tell where someone lives.

I can use math every day.

What Is Counting?

Counting is finding out how many.

I put things together to count them.

I can count the days of the week on a **calendar**.

There are seven days in a week.

What Is Sorting?

Sorting is putting things in groups.

I can sort **counting bears.**

I can sort fruit at home.

I sort apples by color.

What Is a Pattern?

A pattern is the same thing again and again.

We can make a pattern in line.

I make a pattern when I
string beads.

I string red beads, then blue.

What Is a Shape?

A shape is how something looks.

Everything has a shape.

I can draw a shape.

I made a heart for Mom.

What Is a Pair?

A pair is two things that match.

My feet are a pair.

I can make pairs with these socks.

I put the matching socks together.

What Is Telling Time?

hand

Telling time is reading numbers on a clock.

The **hands** show the time.

The hands on this clock show 8:00.

Time to go to school!

What Is Measuring?

When I measure, I find out how big something is.

I can measure with a **ruler**.

I can measure with **counting bears.**

The barn is nine bears long!

How Do I Feel When I Do Math?

I feel proud when I do math.

It makes me feel special.

Doing math makes me
feel important.

When I do math, I can help
other people.

Quiz

What will show how tall you are?

Look for the answer on page 24.

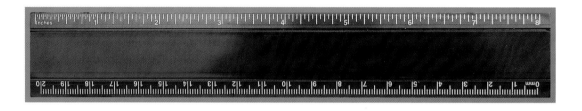

OCTOBER						
		1	2	3	4	5
6	7	8	9	10	11	12
13	14	15	16	17	18	19
20	21	22	23	24	25	26
27	28	29	30	31		

Picture Glossary

calendar
page 7

ruler
page 18

counting bears
pages 8, 19

sorting
pages 8, 9

hands
pages 16, 17

Note to Parents and Teachers

Reading for information is an important part of a child's literacy development. Learning begins with a question about something. Help children think of themselves as investigators and researchers by encouraging their questions about the world around them. Each chapter in this book begins with a question. Read the question together. Look at the pictures. Talk about what you think the answer might be. Then read the text to find out if your predictions were correct. Think of other questions you could ask about the topic, and discuss where you might find the answers. Assist children in using the picture glossary and the index to practice new vocabulary and research skills.

Index

Answer to quiz on page 22

A **ruler** can show how tall you are.